Note to Parents and Teachers

The READING ABOUT: STARTERS series introduces key science vocabulary to young children while encouraging them to discover and understand the world around them. The series works as a set of graded readers in three levels.

LEVEL 2: BEGIN TO READ ALONE follows guidelines set out in the National Curriculum for Year 2 in schools. These books can be read alone or as part of guided or group reading. Each book has three sections:

• Information pages that introduce key words. These key words appear in bold for easy recognition on pages where the related science concepts are explained.
• A lively story that recalls this vocabulary and encourages children to use these words when they talk and write.
• A quiz and index ask children to look back and recall what they have read.

Questions for Further Investigation

HOW BIG IS IT? explains key concepts about MEASURING. Here are some suggestions for further discussion linked to the questions on the information spreads:

p. 5 *What would you use to measure how much you weigh?* e.g. Bathroom scales.

p. 7 *Think of three things you could describe as short, shorter and shortest?* It might help to explain this using simple objects such as pencils of differing lengths.

p. 11 *In your class, who lives nearest to school?* You could also ask children how they travel to school, i.e. people living further away may use a car or bus rather than walk.

p. 13 *What food makes a shopping bag feel heavy?* Vegetables, bags of fruit, tins and bottles can all be heavy. Encourage children to compare the weight of different objects next time they go shopping, e.g. a big packet of cornflakes is surprisingly light.

p. 15 *What other objects would you weigh in tonnes?* Big machines such as trucks, tanks and ships, and very large animals such as whales, rhinos and hippos.

p. 17 *What liquid is put in a car that is measured in litres?* Petrol or diesel. Point out the display on a petrol/diesel pump that shows how many litres are pumped into the car and the display inside the car that shows whether it is full or empty.

p. 19 *Which is longer, the length of a football pitch or the perimeter?* You could ask children to measure a smaller area themselves, e.g. measuring the length and perimeter of a small playground or classroom in paces.

p. 21 *Which do you think is bigger, the area of your hand or foot?* Encourage children to use squared paper to measure this for themselves.

ADVISORY TEAM

Educational Consultant
Andrea Bright – Science Co-ordinator, Trafalgar Junior School, Twickenham

Literacy Consultant
Jackie Holderness – former Senior Lecturer in Primary Education, Westminster Institute, Oxford Brookes University

Series Consultants
Anne Fussell – Early Years Teacher and University Tutor, Westminster Institute, Oxford Brookes University

David Fussell – C.Chem., FRSC

CONTENTS

4   measure, tall, long

6   compare, size, guess

8   length, centimetre, metre

10 distance, kilometre

12 heavy, light, feel

14 weight, gram, kilogram, tonne

16 liquid, litre, millilitre

18 edge, perimeter

20 space, area, square

22 time, speed, heat

24 **Story: The Fancy Dress Party**
Who's put too much chocolate
into the birthday cake?

31 **Quiz**

32 **Index**

© Aladdin Books Ltd 2006

Designed and produced by
Aladdin Books Ltd
2/3 Fitzroy Mews
London W1T 6DF

First published in 2006
in Great Britain
by Franklin Watts
338 Euston Road
London NW1 3BH

Franklin Watts Australia
Hachette Children's Books
Level 17/207 Kent Street
Sydney NSW 2000

ISBN 978 07496 6849 5 (H'bk)
ISBN 978 07496 7030 6 (P'bk)

A catalogue record for this
book is available from the
British Library.
Dewey Classification: 530.8

Printed in Malaysia
All rights reserved

Editor/Designer: Jim Pipe
Series Design: Flick, Book
Design & Graphics

Thanks to:
The pupils of Trafalgar
Infants School, Twickenham, for
appearing as models in this book.

Photocredits:
l-left, r-right, b-bottom, t-top,
c-centre, m-middle
Cover tl & tr, 2tl & bl, 3, 6t,
11tr, 13 both, 14 both, 17b, 18bl,
19, 20tr, 21 both, 24-25 all, 26-
27 all, 28 both, 29tr & mr, 30ml,
31br & bl, 32 — Marc Arundale
/ Select Pictures. Cover tc, 2ml,
6br, 11b, 16b, 31ml — Corbis.
Cover b, 4tl, 5bl, 12t, 15, 16tr,
18tr, 22-23 all, 29bl, 31tr, mr &
bc — istockphoto.com. 44br,
10 both, 12bl — Photodisc. 8
— Corel. 17tr, 18bl — Jim Pipe.
18br — Ingram Publishing. 21
both, 30br — Comstock.

READING ABOUT

Starters

MEASURING

How Big Is It?

By Sally Hewitt

Aladdin/Watts
London • Sydney

Heavy weight

Tall skyscraper

How **tall** is that skyscraper?
How heavy is that weight?

Do you sometimes ask
questions like these?

You can find out the
answers by **measuring**.

We **measure** things in different ways.

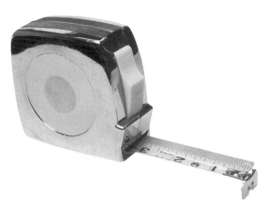

Tape measure

Tape **measures** and rulers **measure** how **long** or **tall** things are.

Scales **measure** how heavy something is.

- What would you use to measure how much you weigh?

Maya   Jenny   Ben

You and your friends can **compare sizes** when you stand next to each other.

Maya is tall.
Jenny is taller.
Ben is the tallest.

Sometimes you can **guess sizes** just by looking.

Can you guess which of these meerkats is the tallest?

6

You can describe the **size** of something by **comparing** it to something else.

How big is this man?

He's bigger than his dog.
He's smaller than his horse.

• Think of three things you could describe as short, shorter and shortest?

The **length** of something is how long it is. You can use all kinds of objects to measure **length**.

The toy truck is four bricks long. It is also six paperclips long.

How many hands long do you think it is?

It helps if we all use the same measurements.

If we measure a book with different bricks or hands, we get different answers.

So we measure the **length** of a book in **centimetres**.

We measure something big like a giraffe in **metres**. There are 100 **centimetres** in a **metre**.

The height of something is how tall it is.

• Can you measure this book in centimetres, using a ruler?

Distance is how far it is between two places, such as your home and your school.

Short **distances** are measured in metres.
A sprint is a short race that is 100 or 200 metres.

A short race

Long **distances** are measured in **kilometres**. You can travel long **distances** by car, train or coach.

Some places are so far away you have to fly there. London to Sydney is 17,000 **kilometres**.

You can use a map to work out the distance between two places.

• In your class, who lives nearest to school?

Big objects are often **heavy**.
A car is made of metal, so it is very **heavy**.
You have to be strong to push it!

These two tubes are big, but they are easy to lift.

They are **light** because they are full of air.

Two objects can look the same size, but they do not weigh the same.

The bag of potatoes **feels heavy**. The bag of popcorn is the same size, but it **feels light**.

A light feather floats down slowly. A heavy marble falls fast.

• What food makes a shopping bag feel heavy?

Kitchen scales

The **weight** of something is how heavy it is.

Kitchen scales measure light objects. They measure **weight** in **grams**.

Bathroom scales measure your **weight** in **kilograms**. There are 1,000 **grams** in a **kilogram**.

Bathroom scales

We use **tonnes** to measure very heavy objects. This elephant **weighs 5 tonnes**.

There are 1,000 **kilograms** in a **tonne.** So the elephant **weighs** 5,000 **kilograms**. It is too heavy to **weigh** on scales!

• What other objects would you weigh in tonnes?

We also measure **liquids**. We use a spoon to measure cooking oil. We can pour a glass of water, but to measure **liquids** exactly, we use **litres**.

A basin holds 4 **litres** of water. A swimming pool holds 50,000 **litres** of water!

Swimming pool

For small amounts of **liquid** we use **millilitres**. There are 1,000 **millilitres** in a **litre**.

These cartons are different shapes but they all hold 500 **millilitres**, or $\frac{1}{2}$ **litre**, of liquid.

Can you guess how much **liquid** this jug holds? It holds 10 glasses of milk.

• What liquid is put in a car that is measured in litres?

If you run all the way round the **edge** of a tennis court, you will have run round the **perimeter**.

The **perimeter** is the outside **edge** of a flat shape such as a table.

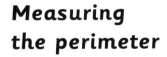
Measuring the perimeter

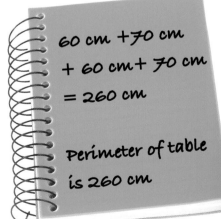

60 cm + 70 cm + 60 cm + 70 cm = 260 cm

Perimeter of table is 260 cm

18

You can use string to measure the **perimeter** of a shape with curved sides.

Pull the string round the **edge** of the shape. Cut the string and measure it with a ruler to find out the **perimeter** of the shape.

• Which is longer, the length of a football pitch or the perimeter?

The **space** inside a flat shape is called the **area**.

We measure **area** in **squares**.

There are lots of little **squares** inside this shape.

Mosaic

Square tiles can help you guess the **area** of a **space** like this kitchen.

Kitchen floor

20

This girl is measuring the **area** of her foot using **squared** paper.

Her friend draws around her foot with a pen.

☐ **This square is 1 square centimetre**

All four sides of the **squares** are 1cm long. So each **square** is one **square** centimetre.

The **area** of this girl's foot is about 12 **square** centimetres.

• *Which do you think is bigger, the area of your hand or foot?*

Clocks and watches measure **time**. School starts at 9 o'clock.

A speedometer measures **speed**. A racing car can **speed** along at over 250 kilometres an hour.

Speedometer

A thermometer measures **heat**.
It tells you the temperature.

Water starts to freeze when the
temperature is 0° Celsius.
You feel very hot when the
temperature is 30° Celsius.

Thermometer

• Can you remember all the different ways we can
measure objects?

THE FANCY DRESS PARTY

*Look out for words about **measuring**.*

Jeff and Saira were excited.
Auntie Fran was coming to stay.
"Here she is now," said Mum.

"You two have grown!"
said Auntie Fran,
giving them a hug.

Guess how **tall** I am!"
said Jeff.
"Um, about a **metre**!"
guessed Auntie Fran.

"We can show you!"
said the children.

24

They **compared** themselves on their **measuring** chart.

"I'm 5 **centimetres taller** than Jeff," said Saira. "And I'm older too!"

They **weighed** themselves on the bathroom scales.

"Saira's **heavier** than me too," sighed Jeff.

"It's my birthday on Saturday. I'm having a fancy dress party."

"Ooh good!" said Auntie Fran. "Can I make the costumes?"

"I'll be a king," said Jeff.
"I'll be a princess," said Saira.

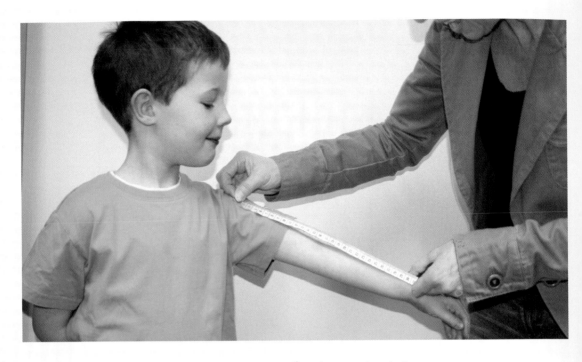

Auntie Fran **measured** the children.
"Now I can make your costumes exactly
the right **size**," she said.

Auntie Fran drew a
pattern using **squared**
paper. "This shows
me the **area**," she said.

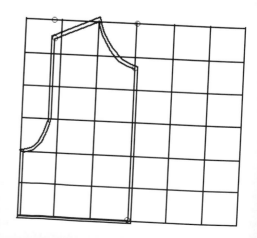

She pinned the pattern to the material and cut round the **edges** of the shapes.

Then she sewed the **long** pieces of material together.

The children tried on their costumes.

"Cool!" said Jeff.

"I love my dress!" said Saira. "It's just the right **length.**"

Some of the guests arrived early. They helped Mum make the birthday cake.

Jeff **weighed** the ingredients on the kitchen scales.

When nobody was looking, Clare put in an extra 50 **grams** of chocolate chips.

When David mixed the ingredients, he put in an extra 50 **grams** of chocolate chips too!

Mum turned on the **heat** and put the cake in the oven. Auntie Fran filled a big jug with juice.

"This jug **feels heavy**," said Jeff.

"One **litre** of juice is about enough for 8 cups," said Auntie Fran.

When all the party guests had arrived, everyone played games in the garden.

There was plenty of **space** to run around fast.

"Tea **time**!" called Auntie Fran. They all sat round the table. Mum brought in the cake.

"This cake feels like it **weighs** a **tonne**!" she said. "What did you children put in it?" David and Clare giggled.

Everyone agreed it was the best chocolate cake they had ever tasted.

Cut out and colour 5 outlines of your foot. Stick them on a long strip of paper.

Now use this to **measure** things around your house, such as a dog or teddy bear.

This dog is 3 "feet" tall

QUIZ

What do we use to **measure** how **heavy** something is?

Answer on page 5

What do we **measure** long **distances** in?

Answer on page 11

What does a thermometer **measure**?

Answer on page 23

Which of these things would you measure in tonnes, which in litres and which in kilograms?

Have you read this book? Well done! Do you remember these words? Look back and find out.

INDEX

A
area 20

C
centimetre 8
compare 6

D
distance 10

E
edge 18

F
feel 12

G
gram 14
guess 6

H
heat 22
heavy 12

K
kilogram 14
kilometre 10

L
length 8
light 12
liquid 16
litre 16
long 4

M
measure 4
metre 8
millilitre 16

P
perimeter 18

S
size 6
space 20
speed 22
square 20

T
tall 4
time 22
tonne 14

W
weight 14